Contents

Foreword

By Joseph E. Stiglitz

Recipient of the Nobel Memorial Prize in Economic Sciences, 2001,
and University Professor at Columbia University in New York

The election of Donald Trump as president of the United States in November, 2016, was greeted with great concern around the world. How could the US – a country heralded as the leader of the free world – have chosen a leader who was openly racist, bigoted, and misogynistic, with a predilection for authoritarian leaders and a seeming disdain for democratic values and institutions, including a free press? There was a widespread hope that after assuming the presidency the gravity of the office would induce Trump to act more responsibly, or that perhaps his party would rein him in. But the country and the world got what they had dreaded – and worse. In office, Trump was as deceptive and deceitful as he had seemed on the campaign trail, with the same disdain for honesty and truth. Indeed, this is perhaps the only thing to his credit: He did not mislead voters about his habitual deceptiveness or his other horrendous traits.

To many Americans, every day was anguish, and the only salve for our pain was Chappatte's cartoons, with their satire and humor. His cartoons could help us come to terms with what was happening, even, perhaps, help us better understand our anguish. How else do you deal with something as grotesque, ridiculous, and unbelievable, but nonetheless real and consequential?

> *"To many Americans, every day was anguish, and the only salve for our pain was Chappatte's cartoons"*

These cartoons became the way we collectively could deal with what was befalling the country. We could share the cartoons with each other, communicating our feelings more poignantly, more forcefully, than any assemblage of words. As Chappatte has put it, "We as humans need humor as much as the air we breathe. In this day and age, it's needed more than ever."

This, of course, has been the role of political cartoons and satire for a long time. Indeed, cartoons of an earlier era are part of what helps us understand the nature of political discourse of past years. Men "of importance," with outsized egos, whose assessments of themselves are so detached from reality, need to be deflated – somebody has to prick a hole in the bubble they create around themselves, especially since they are inevitably surrounded by sycophants. Someone has to show that the emperor has no clothes, and to do it in a way that doesn't resort to the same pomposity that characterizes these men of power. Good cartoons have always done this, and for our troubled time, no one reflects this time-honored tradition better than Chappatte.

In the case of Trump, the challenge of providing a compelling cartoon caricature is all the more difficult, partly because Trump is a caricature of himself, and partly because it's seldom clear what Trump is standing for – he can be both for and against the same thing at the same time. Chappatte's cartoons are able even to capture and satirize these contradictions.

It's hard to know whether political cartoons like these convince Trump's supporters of his follies. At the very least, they should make them think twice about their blind support. Cartoons have long spoken truth to power, and the clarity they provide is often uncomfortable for those in control who would like to suppress, or at least, distort, the truth.

In badly divided societies such as the US and many other countries these days, satirical cartoons sometimes seem to stretch norms – about what can and cannot be said in public. With a president who violates norms on a daily basis, it is understandable that there should be nervousness about a further stretching. But there is a fundamental difference between the crude and coarse norm-breaking of Trump and the targeted, reasoned norm-breaking associated with satirical cartoons. It was wrong, I believe, for *The New York Times* to stop running cartoons simply because in this age of political correctness, some thin-skinned readers might be offended.

That's one of the reasons why the publication of Chappatte's cartoons together in a collection is so important. Here we see both Chappatte and Trump in all their dimensions, one clever, subtle, witty, pointed – everything that we value in the best of political cartoons – and the other, well… Chappatte best describes the nightmare.

Chapter 1

Trumpland

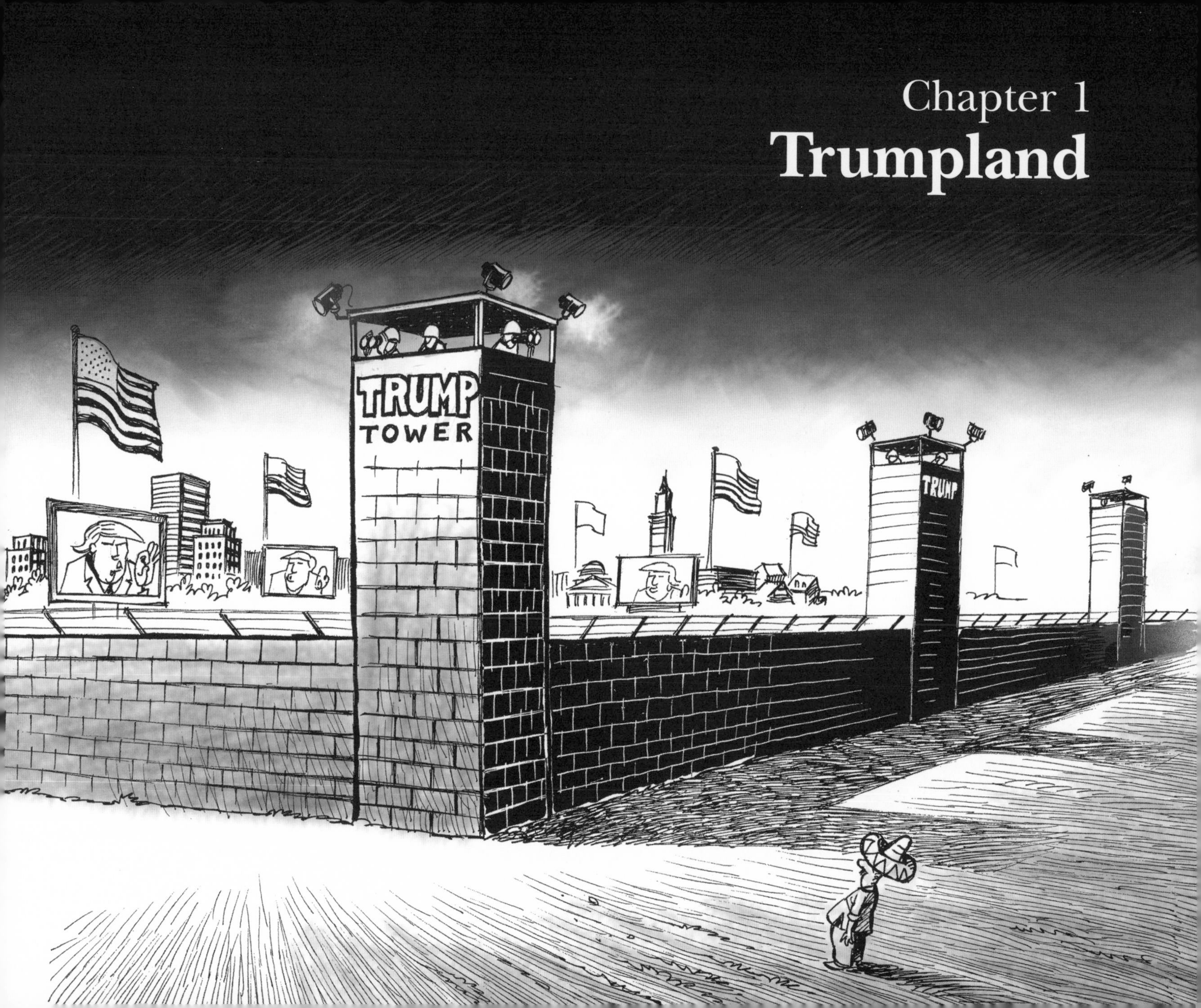
TRUMP TOWER
TRUMP

The new leader of the free world

December 24, 2016

Donald about women: "When you're a star,
you can grab'em by the pussy"

October 12, 2016

The 45th president of the United States
takes the oath on January 20, 2017

January 21, 2017

Donald Trump claims his inauguration crowd
was larger than Obama's – which is not true

February 21, 2018

The travel ban for visitors from six predominantly Muslim nations
announces a new immigration policy

February 1st, 2017

As his travel ban is scrutinized in courts,
Trump attacks "so-called judges"

February 8, 2017

Trump wants to renegotiate
trade agreements with China

January 26, 2017

The president calls some US media "fake news"
and "enemy of the people"

March 2, 2017

FBI's James Comey, criticized for his handling
of the Hillary Clinton email controversy, testifies on
Russian interference in the US election

March 22, 2017

In May 2017, special counsel Robert Mueller
is appointed to investigate Russia's links to
the Trump presidential campaign

May 20, 2017

Trump's campaign pledge to repeal and
replace Obamacare fails in Congress

March 29, 2017

Trump signs executive orders undercutting
Obama's Affordable Care Act

October 18, 2017

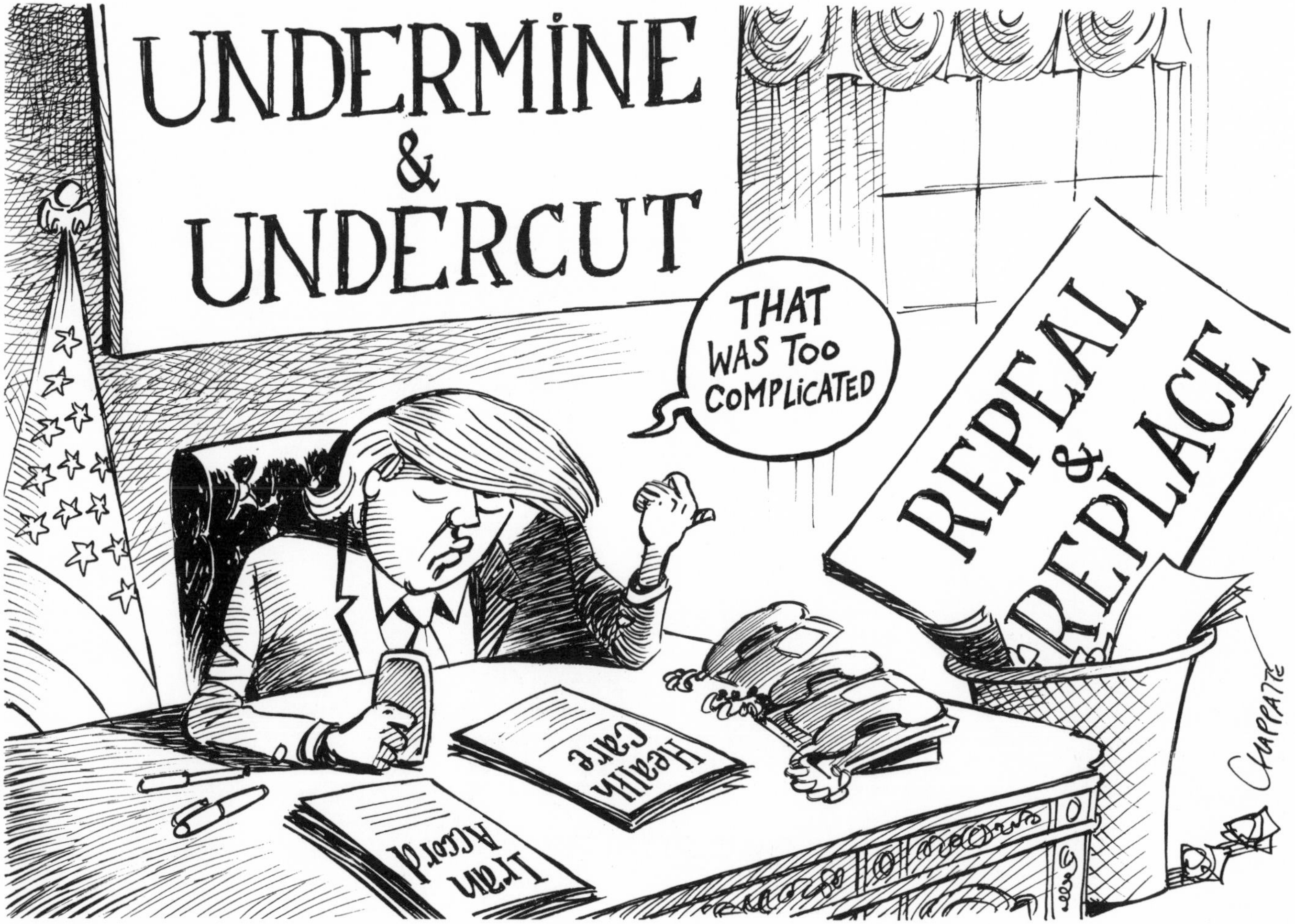
UNDERMINE
&
UNDERCUT
THAT WAS TOO COMPLICATED
REPEAL & REPLACE
Health Care
Iran Accord
CHAPPATTE

18

Trump pulls out of the Paris climate accord,
adopted by nearly 200 countries

April 4, 2017

Hurricane Harvey hits Texas and Louisiana,
causing catastrophic flooding and many deaths

September 2, 2017

WannaCry ransomware worm wreaks havoc worldwide,
using tools stolen from the National Security Agency

May 17, 2017

Amazon acquires Whole Foods
and has big ambitions in grocery

June 21, 2017

White supremacist rally in Charlottesville results in the death
of a counter-demonstrator. Trump blames "both sides"

August 16, 2017

The Republican Party

August 28, 2017

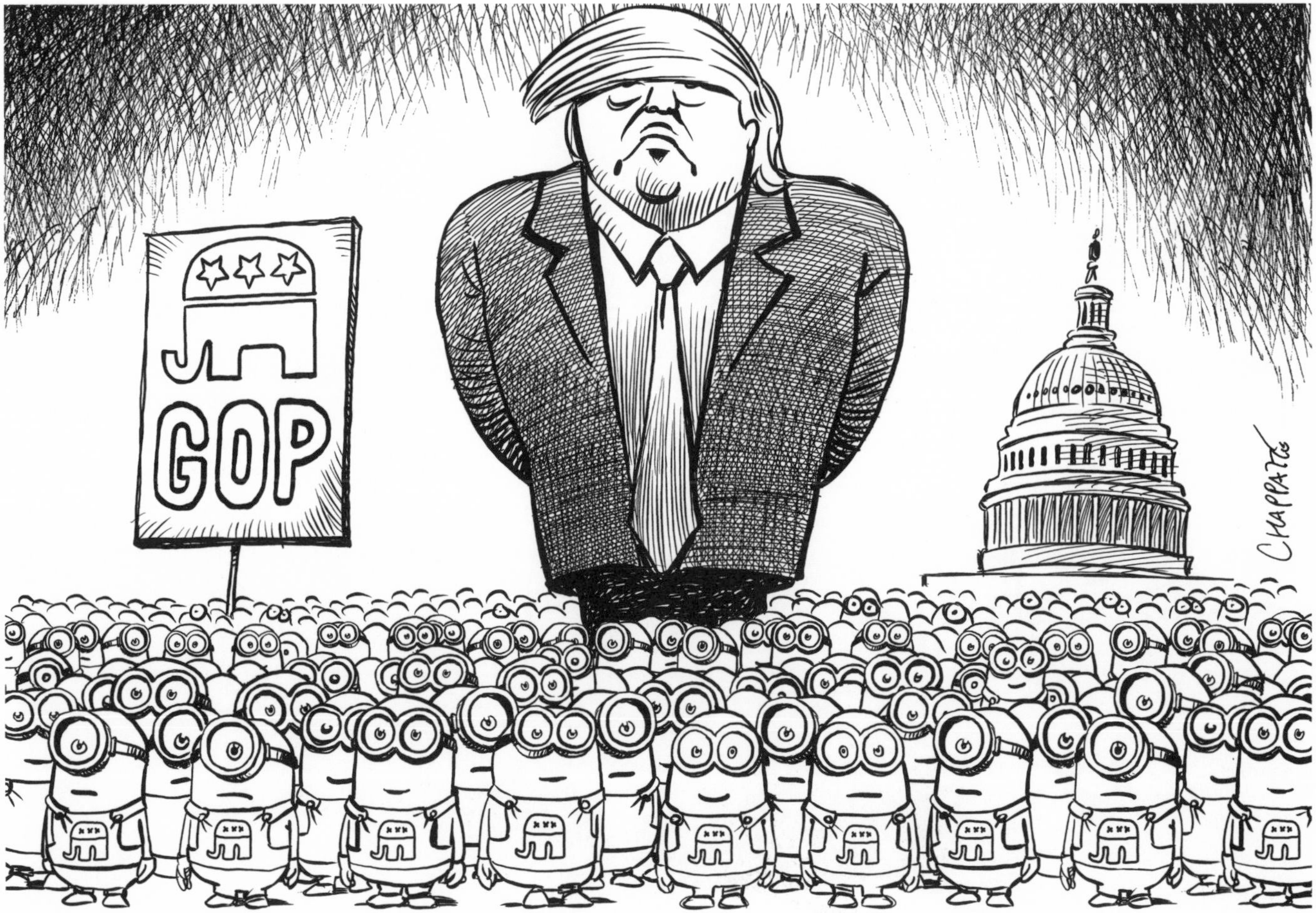
GOP
CHAPPATTE

American film mogul Harvey Weinstein is accused
of rape and sexual abuse by dozens of women

October 14, 2017

Weinstein scandal triggers #MeToo movement for women's rights,
sexual harassment cases soar

December 30, 2017

Just in for Christmas: a sweeping tax cut for the rich

December 20, 2017

The new tax cut package reduces corporate
tax rate to 21%, from 35%

December 13, 2017

The president repeatedly calls himself "a very stable genius"

January 10, 2018

"Why should we take immigrants from shithole countries – rather than places like Norway?", asks Trump

January 17, 2018

March for Our Lives, a massive student-led demonstration in
support of gun control legislation, fails to convince Congress to act

March 24, 2018

February 24, 2018

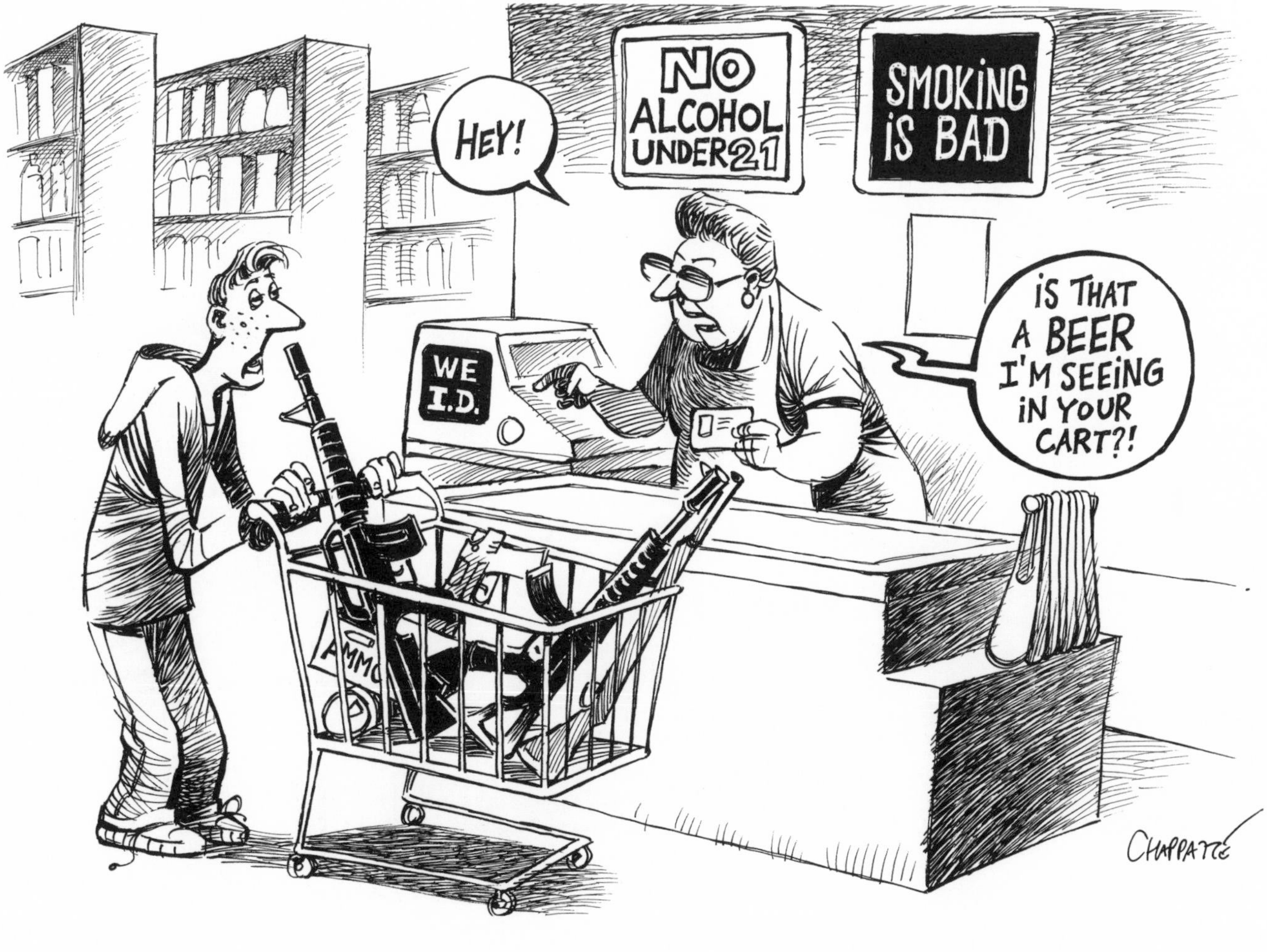
HEY!
NO ALCOHOL UNDER 21
SMOKING IS BAD
WE I.D.
IS THAT A BEER I'M SEEING IN YOUR CART?!
AMMO
CHAPPATTE

The White House keeps a close eye
on the Russian investigation

January 31, 2018

Former New York mayor Rudolph W. Giuliani becomes
Trump's top lawyer – and surrogate

May 9, 2018

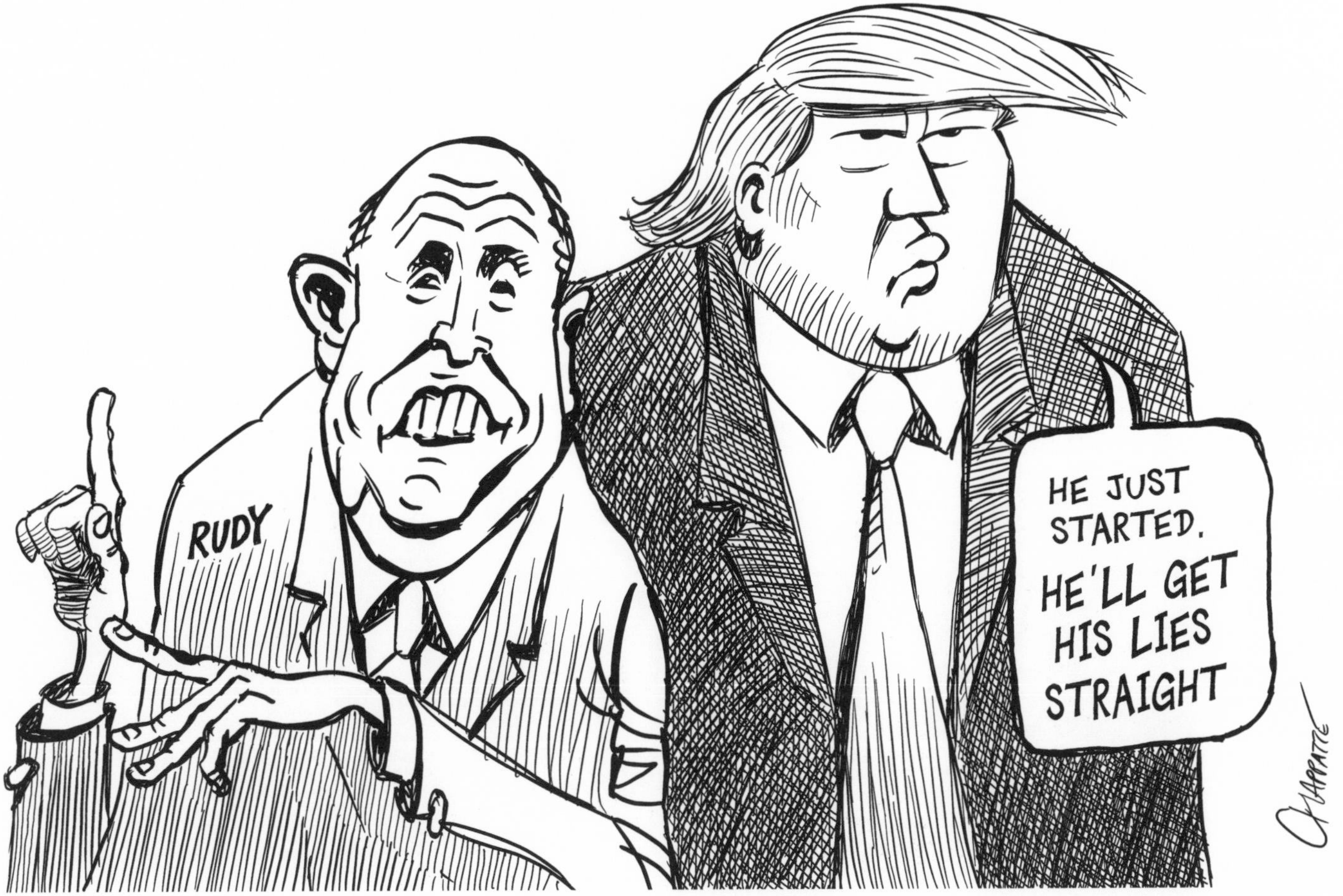
RUDY
HE JUST STARTED.
HE'LL GET HIS LIES STRAIGHT
CHAPPATTE

The Fed scales back restrictions on certain types of risky trading
that were introduced after the 2008 financial crisis

June 6, 2018

Trade war between the US and China

Porn actress Stormy Daniels was paid $130,000.00 before the 2016 election to keep silent about an affair she had with Trump – a campaign finance violation

April 18, 2018

After Justice Anthony Kennedy's retirement, Trump ponders
his second Supreme Court Justice nomination

June 30, 2018

Federal authorities start separating children from parents
with whom they have entered the US illegally

June 26, 2018

The Trump administration family separation policy

June 20, 2018

Ten years after the 2008 financial collapse,
bank rules are being relaxed

September 15, 2018

Climate change protests multiply

October 10, 2018

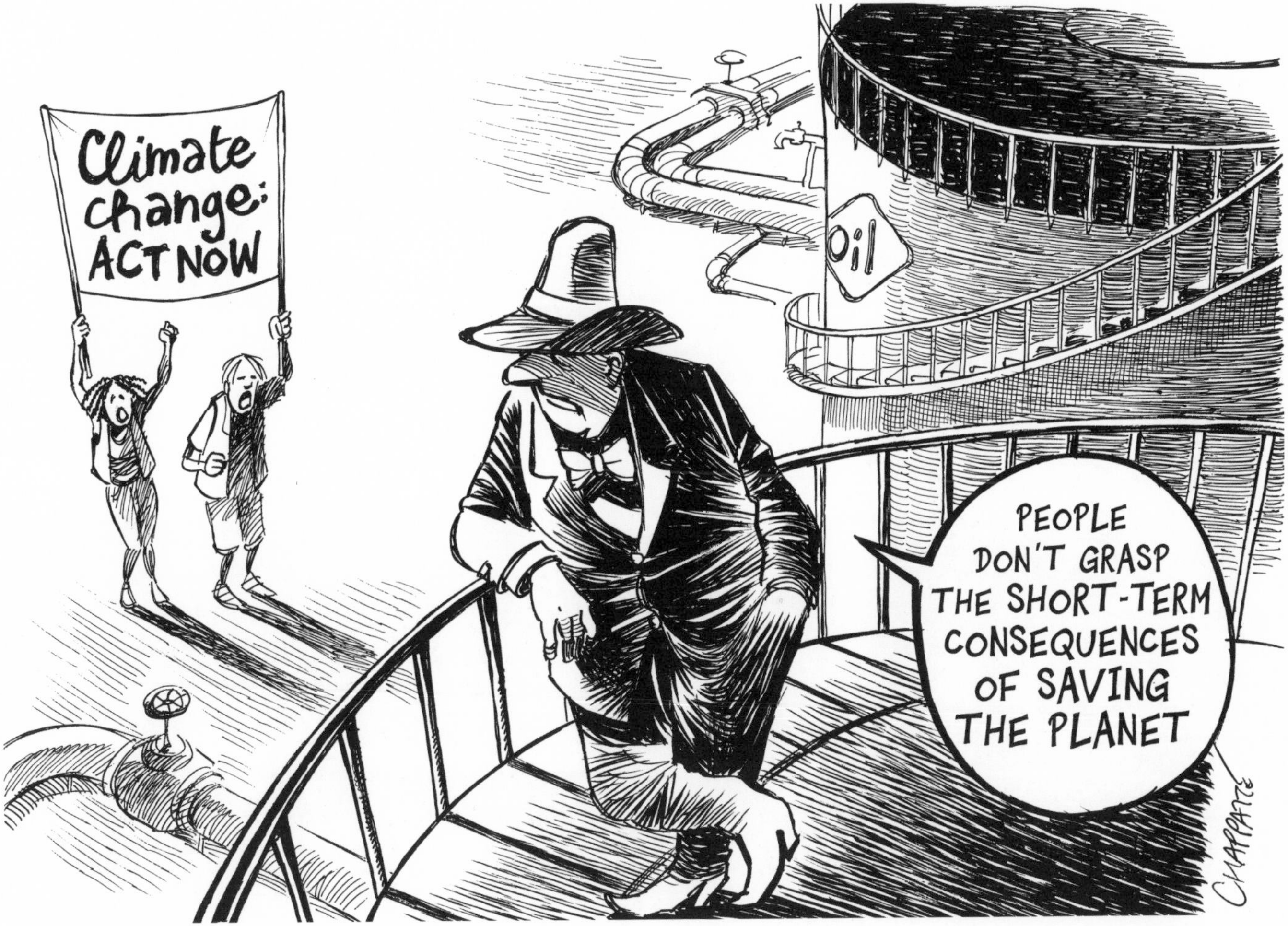
Climate change: ACT NOW
Oil
PEOPLE DON'T GRASP THE SHORT-TERM CONSEQUENCES OF SAVING THE PLANET
CHAPPATTE

After a wave of mail bombs targeting prominent Trump critics,
like George Soros, the president condemns the acts

October 27, 2018

Brett Kavanaugh is confirmed at the Supreme Court, following bitter Senate hearings over accusations of sexual misconduct

October 6, 2018

Midterm elections take place in a divided country

November 6, 2018

The Democratic Party gains a majority
in the US House of Representatives

November 8, 2018

California is plagued by severe drought and repeated wildfires

December 1st, 2018

The administration presses on with plans
for a Mexico border wall

January 12, 2019

The US government bans tech giant Huawei, arguing its equipment could be used by the Chinese authorities to spy on communications

March 9, 2019

When will the Boeing 737 MAX fly again? It was grounded after two deadly crashes linked to its automated flight-control system

March 14, 2019

The Mueller Report on Russia "does not conclude that
the President committed a crime" (of obstruction)
but "it also does not exonerate him"

April 20, 2019

Attorney General William Barr is accused of
acting like the president's personal lawyer

April 4, 2019

One more: national security adviser John Bolton is fired

September 14, 2019

Record turnover in the Trump administration

March 3, 2018

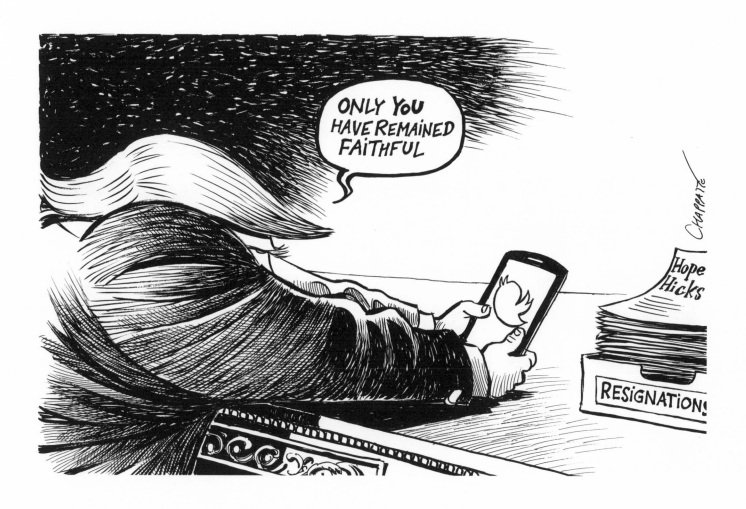

Donald Trump has never made his tax returns public,
despite promising on several occasions to do so

May 10, 2019

Impeachment inquiry: Trump is accused of pressuring Ukraine's
president to find dirt on a political opponent, Joe Biden

September 29, 2019

Trump's problematic phone calls with foreign leaders

October 5, 2019

A lasting legacy...

October 10, 2019

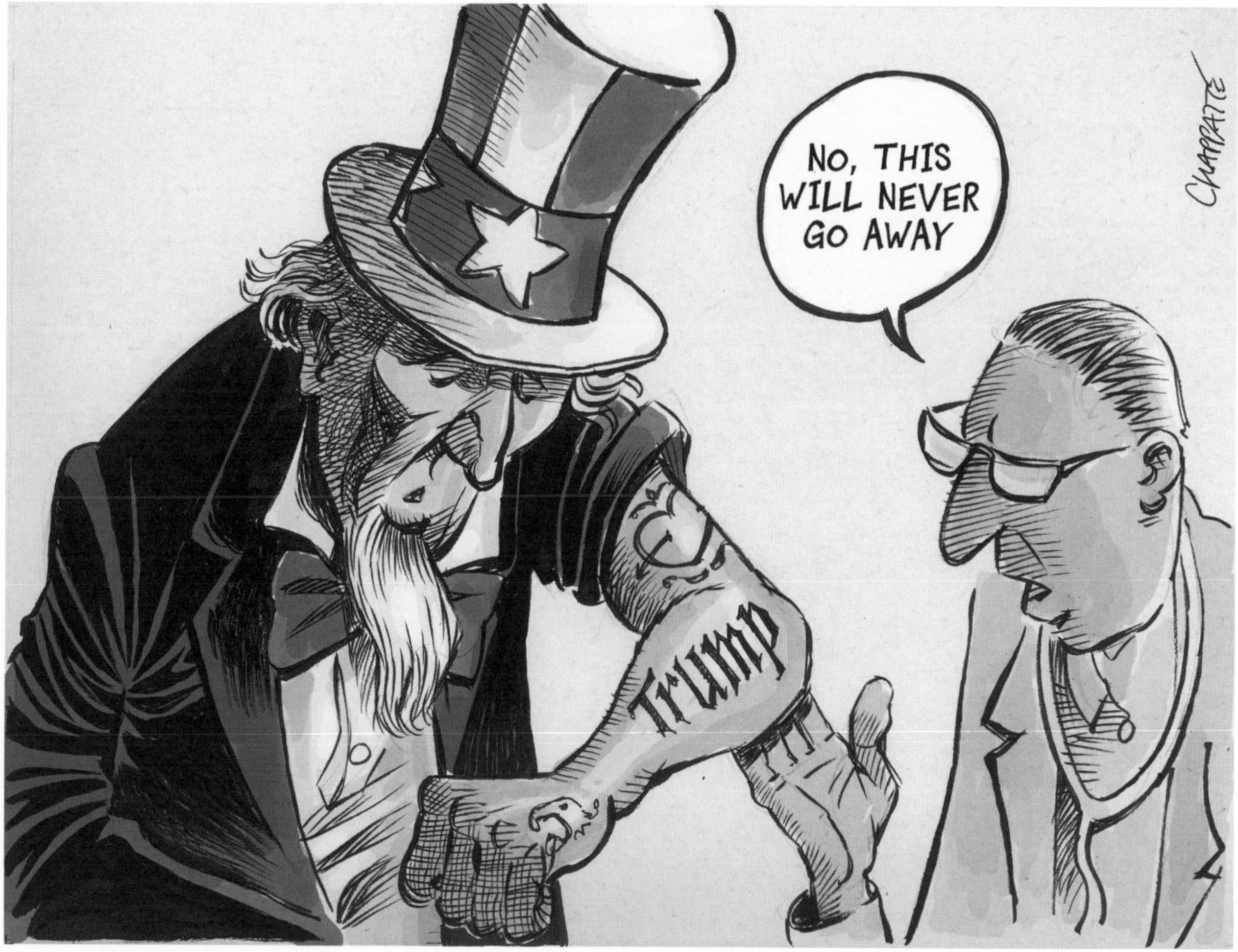
No, THIS
WILL NEVER
GO AWAY
Trump
CHAPPATTE

Chapter 2
Rest of the (Trump) World

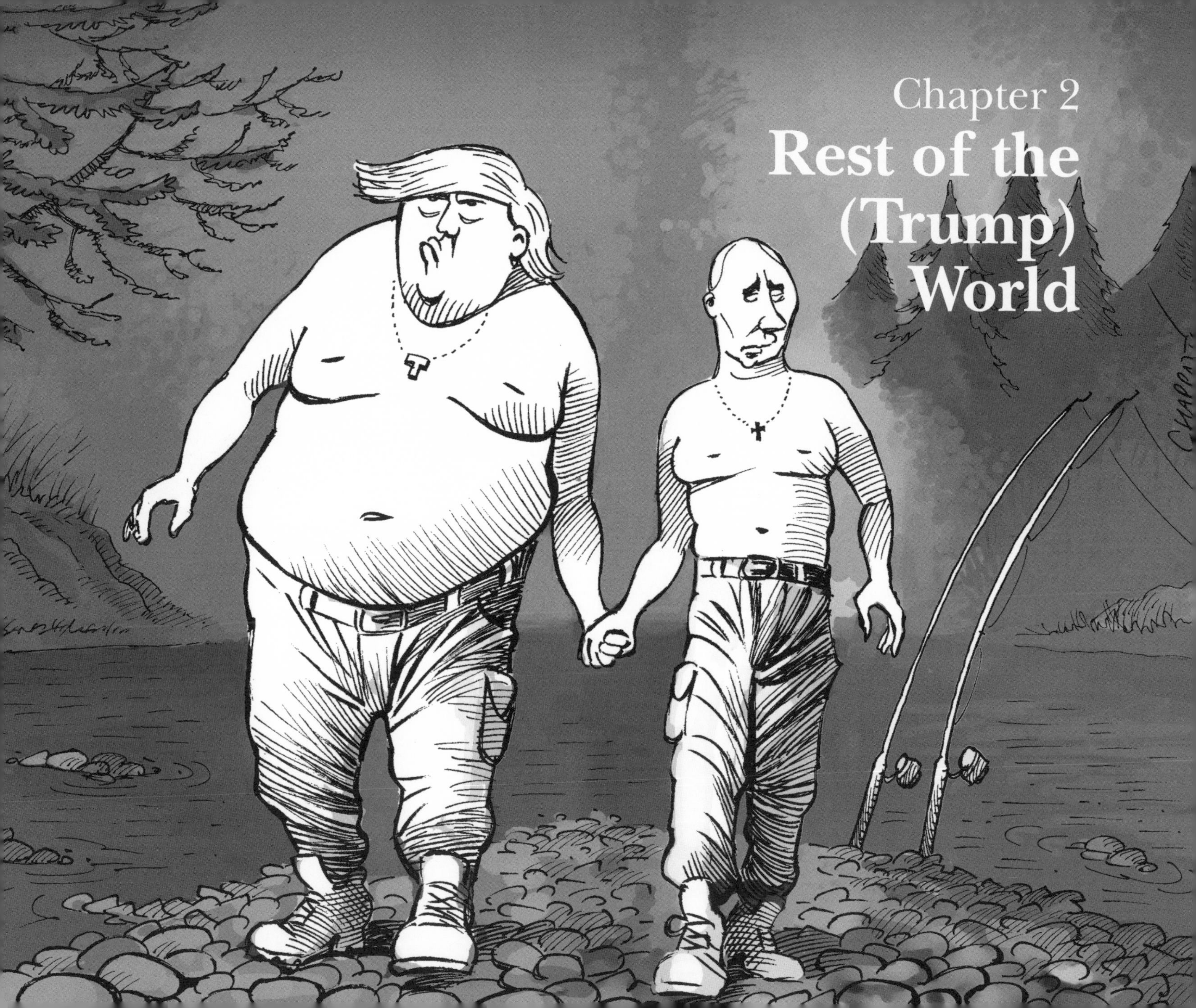

In a Europe shaken by Brexit and the rise of populism,
Angela Merkel holds on

November 23, 2016

The president of the United States meets the
German chancelor at the White House

March 15, 2017

Vice-president Mike Pence tries to convince a wary Europe
of the US's continued committment to Nato

February 22, 2017

With the help of Russia, Assad takes back Aleppo

December 3, 2016

Beating the far-right contender Marine Le Pen,
Emmanuel Macron becomes president of France

May 9, 2017

Trump meets Pope Francis at the Vatican

May 27, 2017

Trump's first foreign visit is to Saudi Arabia

May 24, 2017

Finally, Saudi women are allowed to drive

September 30, 2017

Spain tries to stop (illegal) Catalan independence
referendum, leaving hundreds of people injured

October 4, 2017

The most expensive painting ever sold

November 18, 2017

Mohammed bin Salman, Saudi Arabia's
adventurous crown prince

November 15, 2017

The fall of its capital Raqqa marks
the demise of the Islamic State

October 21, 2017

Trump recognizes Jerusalem as the capital of Israel,
the UN General Assembly condemns the decision

December 23, 2017

As Ivanka and Jared Kushner inaugurate Jerusalem embassy,
Israeli forces kill dozens of Palestinians protesting in Gaza

May 16, 2018

After courting Trump in Paris, Macron visits him in Washington

April 25, 2018

G7 summit in Canada marked by diagreements

June 9, 2018

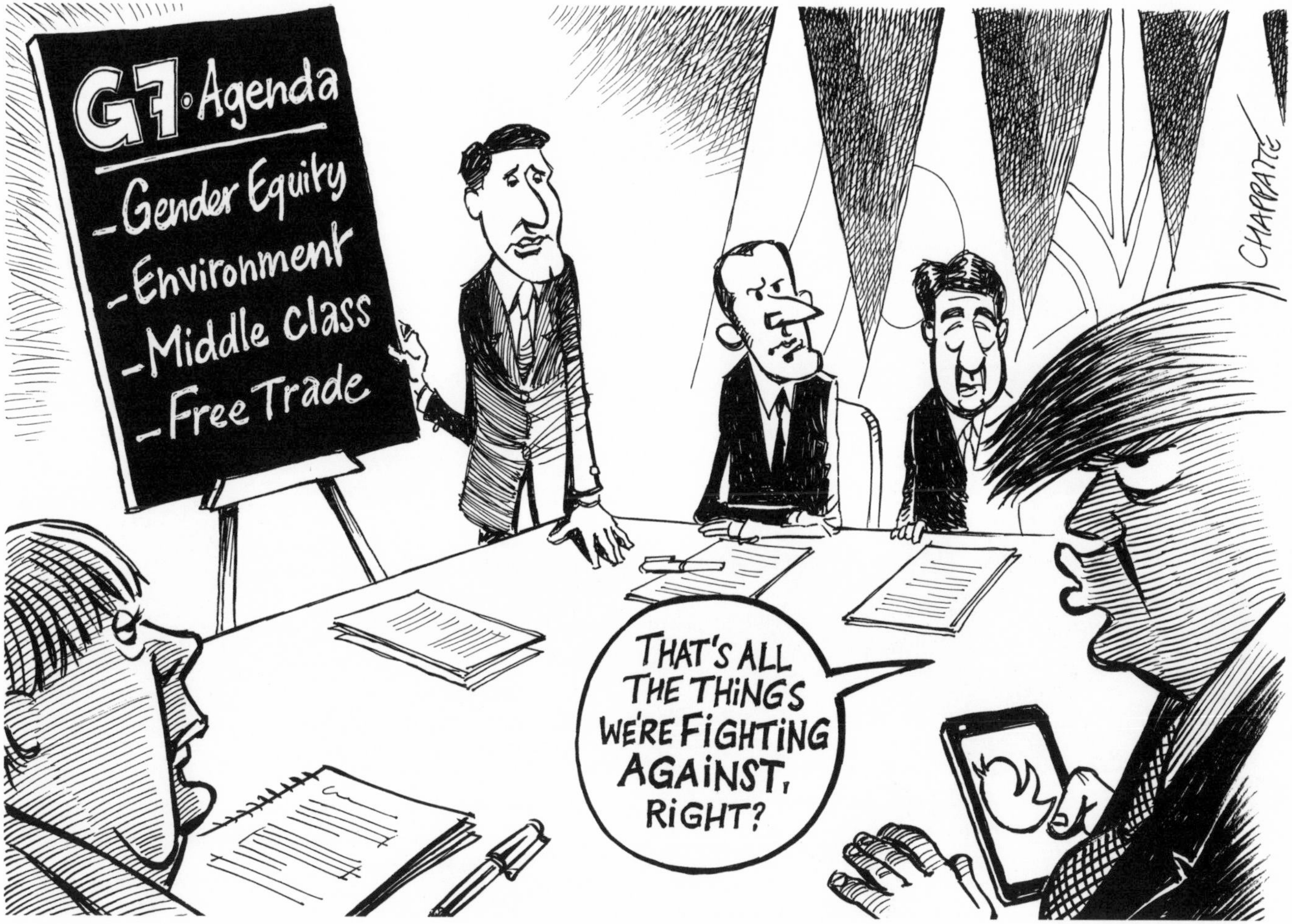
G7 Agenda
- Gender Equity
- Environment
- Middle Class
- Free Trade
THAT'S ALL THE THINGS WE'RE FIGHTING AGAINST, RIGHT?
CHAPPATTE

The US exits the Iran nuclear deal reached by world powers
in 2015 to control Tehran's nuclear program

May 12, 2018

Hope for peace: for the first time, a North Korean leader steps into the South for an inter-Korean summit

April 28, 2018

Trump meets Kim Jong-un in Singapore, the first-ever meeting
between leaders of North Korea and the US

June 12, 2018

Left-wing leader Andrés Manuel López Obrador
becomes the president of Mexico

July 4, 2018

The US doubles metal tariffs on Turkey

August 15, 2018

Two American presidents

July 14, 2018

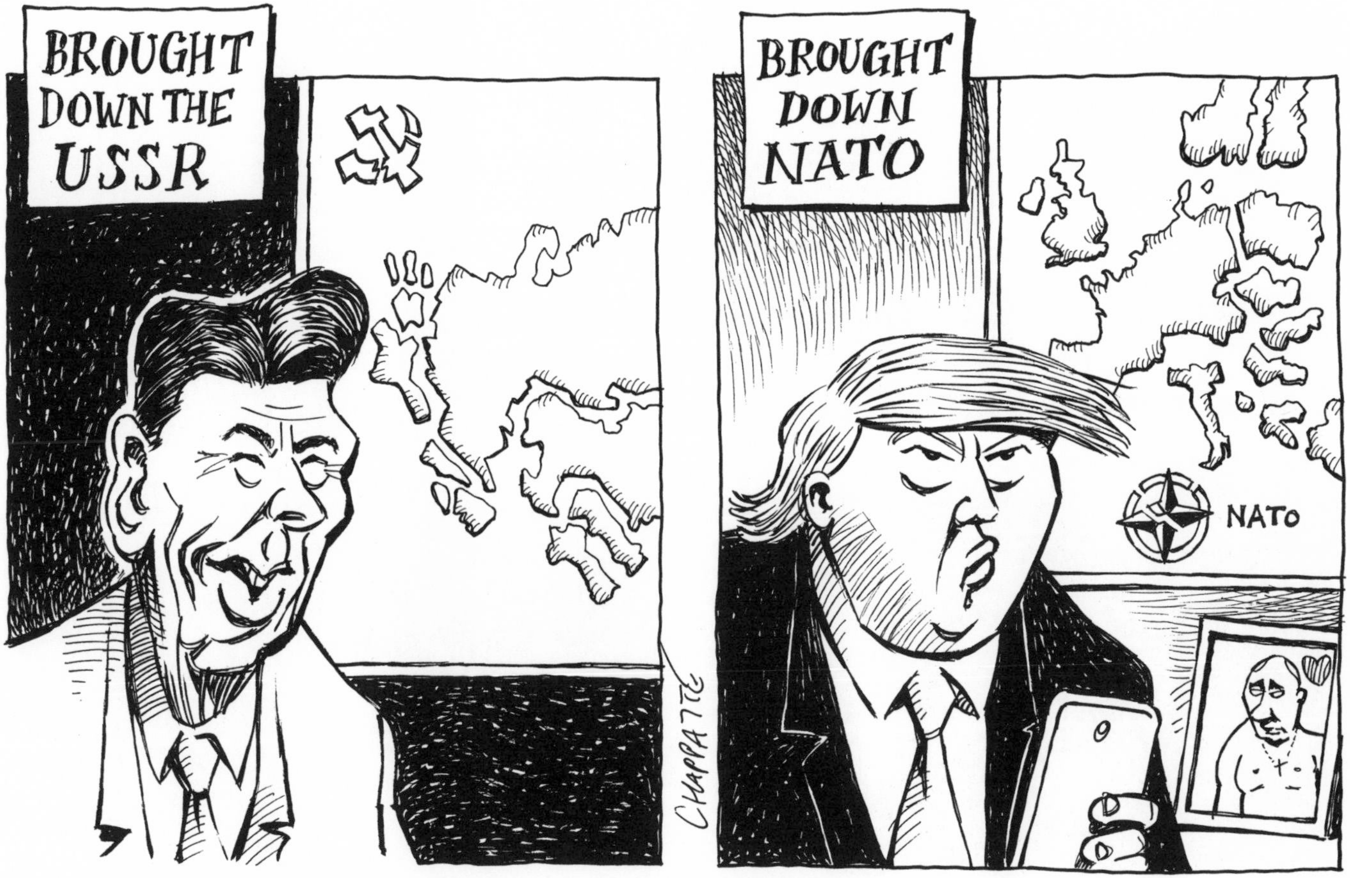
BROUGHT DOWN THE USSR
BROUGHT DOWN NATO
NATO
CHAPPATTE

Pennsylvania grand jury report finds that more than
1000 children have been abused by Catholic clergy

August 18, 2018

After a 3-year European bailout program,
Greece is on its own

August 22, 2018

Trump halts funding to UN agency
helping Palestinian refugees

September 5, 2018

Bashar al-Assad, victor of the Syrian war

September 12, 2019

Life in the era of facial recognition

May 25, 2019

Mark Zuckerberg is your friend.
(Meanwhile, Facebook collects thousands of data points
from users and seeks to monetize them.)

April 15, 2018

Famine in Venezuela under president Maduro's rule

August 29, 2018

The US backs Nicolás Maduro's opponent Juan Guaidó,
who declares himself the legitimate president of Venezuela

February 2, 2019

Prince Salman, the Saudi reformer? The brutal killing of opponent Jamal Khashoggi ruins the myth

October 13, 2018

Trump stands by the Saudi prince and
resists calls to end US support of Yemen war

October 17, 2018

Far-right candidate and dictatorship apologist
Jair Bolsonaro is the new ruler of Brazil

October 30, 2018

100 years after World War I

November 14, 2018

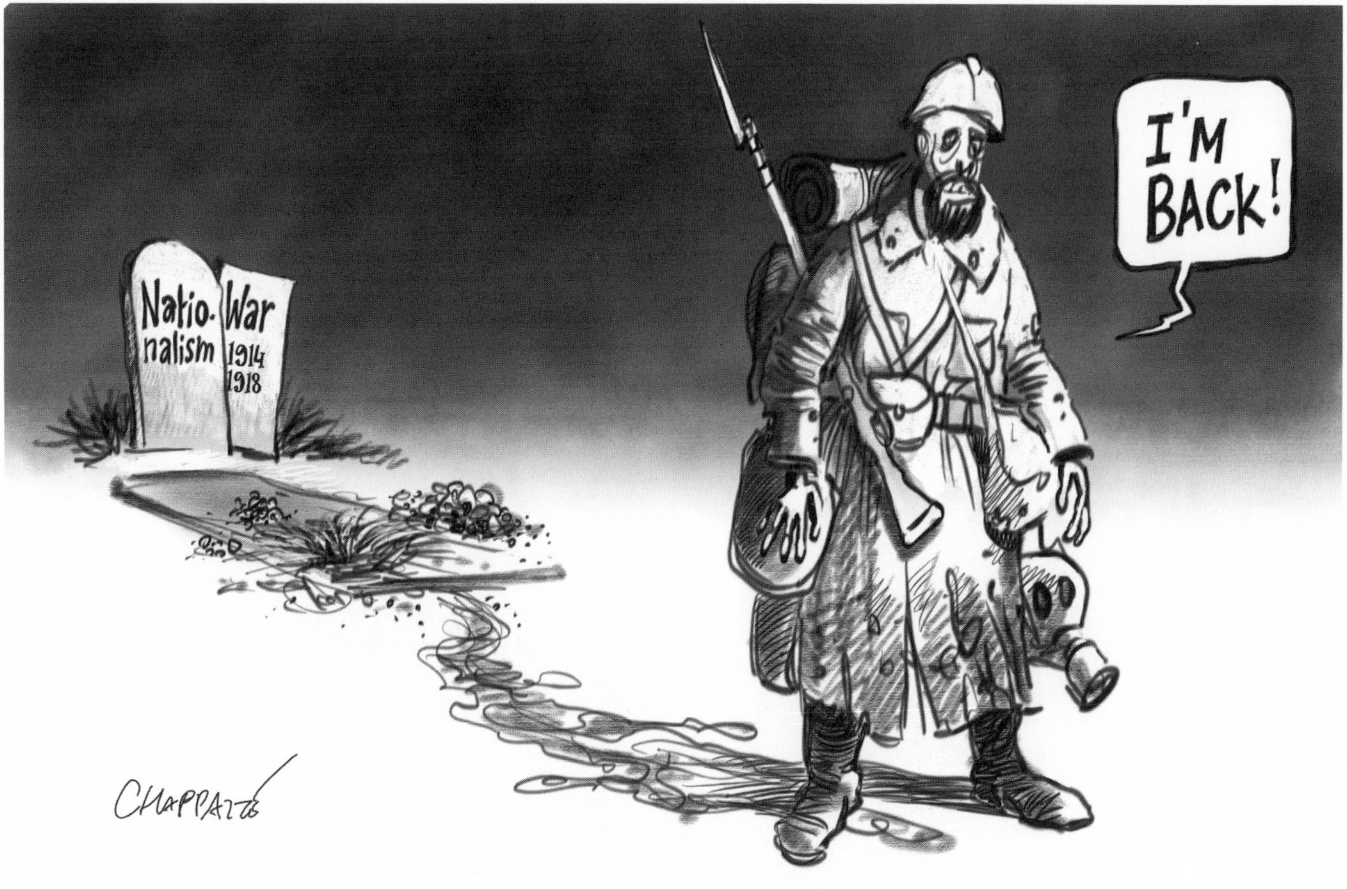
Natio-nalism
War 1914 1918
I'M BACK!
CHAPPATTE

A more assertive China challenges the US in Asia

November 28, 2018

Brexit debate after Brexit debate
in the Bitish parliament

December 15, 2018

The second Trump-Kim meeting takes place in Hanoi

February 27, 2019

Trump walks out of the North Korea summit with no agreement

March 6, 2019

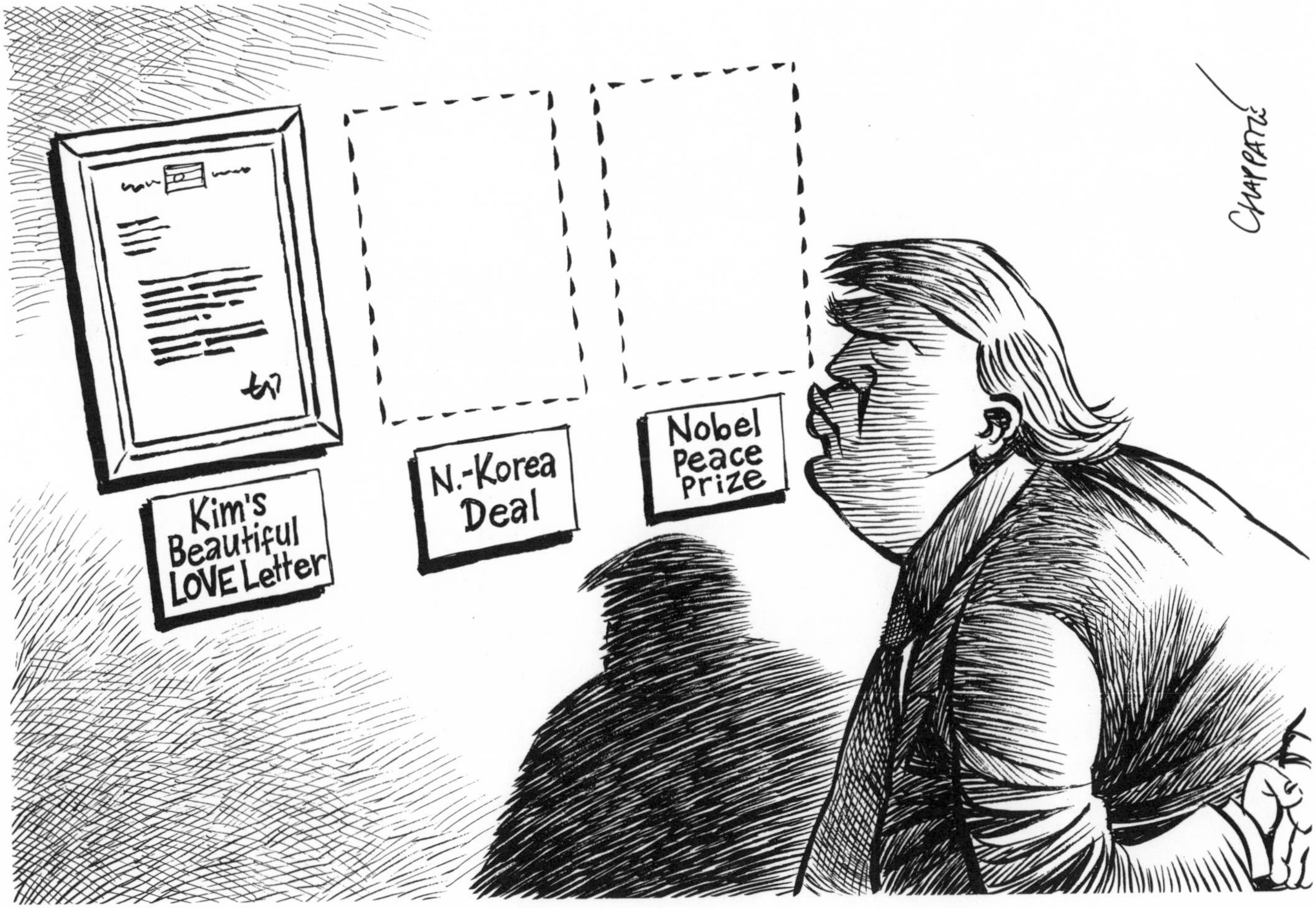
Kim's Beautiful LOVE Letter
N.-Korea Deal
Nobel Peace Prize
CHAPPATTE

40 years after its Islamic revolution,
Iran faces growing pressure from the US

February 13, 2019

Months of mass protests in Algeria bring an end to
Abdelaziz Bouteflika's reign of nearly 20 years

April 6, 2019

Communist party cadres across China are required
to use propaganda app every day – and earn points!

April 10, 2019

The emperor of Japan Akihito steps down
in first abdication in two centuries

May 2, 2019

Time to act on climate change

December 8, 2018

Time to act on climate change

September 4, 2019

...And more Brexit debate after Brexit debate after Brexit debate after Brexit debate after Brexit debate after Brexit debate...

January 25, 2019

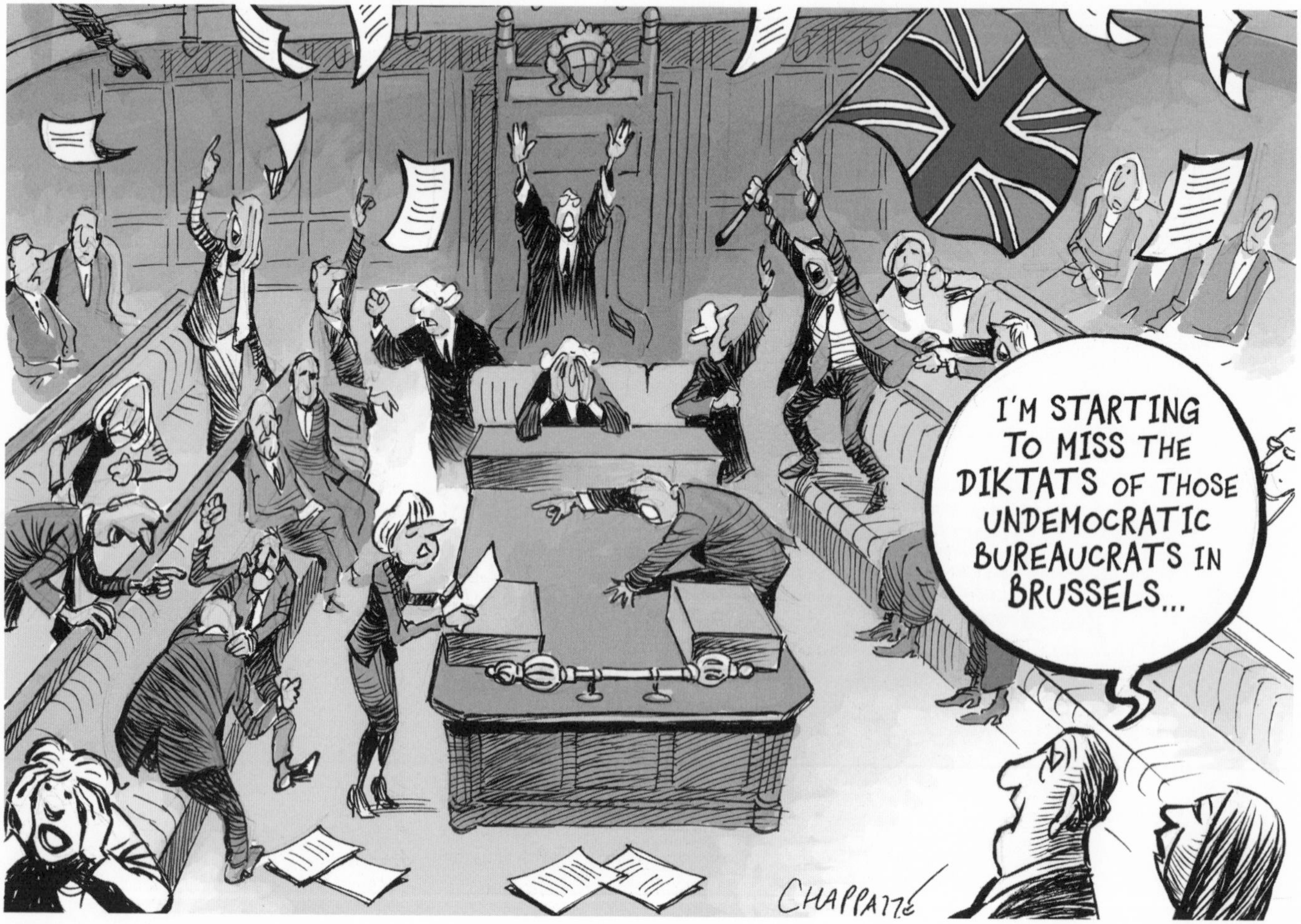
I'M STARTING TO MISS THE DIKTATS OF THOSE UNDEMOCRATIC BUREAUCRATS IN BRUSSELS...
CHAPPATTE

Trump cancels a visit to Denmark
over the country's refusal to cede Greenland,
and meets his new friend Boris Johnson

August 28, 2019

Trump orders troops out of Northern Syria,
abandoning the Kurds to a Turkish invasion

October 10, 2019

After the abandonment of the Kurds,
friends of the US are left wondering

October 10, 2019

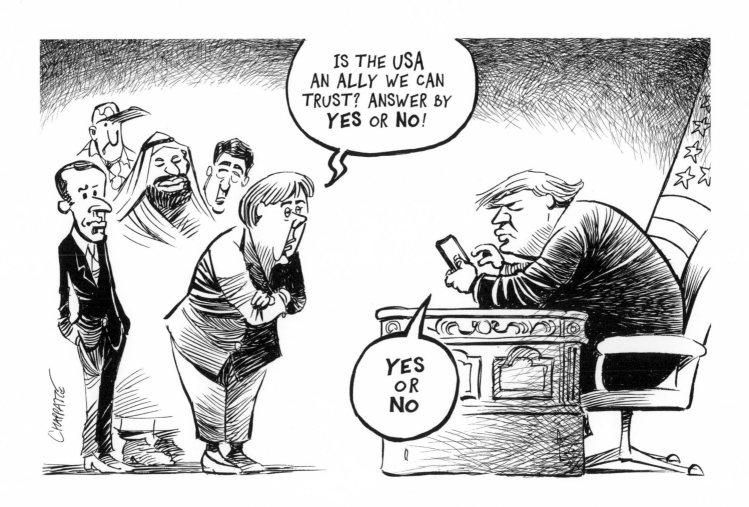

The End of Political Cartoons at *The New York Times*

By Patrick Chappatte

All my professional life, I have been driven by the conviction that the unique freedom of political cartooning entails a great sense of responsibility.

For the last 20 years, I had been with the *International Herald Tribune*, and then *The New York Times*, delivering a twice-weekly cartoon for the Opinion section. But in April 2019, something happened. A syndicated cartoon distributed by an agency was picked by a *NYT* editor and put on the Opinion page. This thing blew up. Initially published by the newspaper *Expresso* in Lisbon, the caricature by António Moreira Antunes, a famous Portuguese artist, did not go well in the columns of the *Times*: it was quickly denounced as anti-Semitic, triggered widespread outrage, apologies and a lot of damage control by the newspaper. Weeks later, my editor told me they were ending political cartoons altogether.

That cartoon was debatable, to say the least. Some people said it reminded them of anti-Semitic propaganda. Others, including in Israel, replied no, it was just a harsh criticism of Trump – who was depicted as the blind follower of Israel's prime minister. I had some issues with that image. (You can check it for yourself by googling "*NYT* Netanyahu cartoon".) But there was no such discussion in *The New York Times*. Under attack, they took the easiest route: to avoid problems with political cartoons in the future, let's not have any at all. Hey, this is new: did we just invent preventive self-censorship? I'm afraid this is bigger than cartoons. It's about opinion and journalism in general. In the end, it's about democracy.

> *"Political cartoons were born with democracy. And they are challenged when freedom is."*

Along with *The Economist*, featuring the excellent Kal, *The New York Times* was one of the last venues for international political cartooning. Cartoons can jump over borders. Who will show the emperor Erdogan that he has no clothes, when Turkish cartoonists can't do it? – one of them, Musa Kart, was sent to jail. Cartoonists from Venezuela, Nicaragua and Russia have been forced into exile. In the United States, over the last years, some of the very best cartoonists, like Nick Anderson and Rob Rogers, lost their positions. The latter was fired because his editor found his work too critical of Trump. Something similar happened to Canadian cartoonist Michael De Hadder. Maybe we should start worrying. Political cartoons were born with democracy. And they are challenged when freedom is.

We now live in a world where moralistic mobs gather on social media and rise like a storm. The most outraged voices tend to define the conversation, and the angry crowd follows in. These social media storms, sometimes triggered by special interest groups, fall upon newsrooms in an overwhelming blow, and send publishers scrambling for countermeasures. This leaves no room for meaningful discussions. Twitter is a place for fury, not for debate.

Social media exposure is both a blessing and a curse for political cartoons. They are an encapsulated opinion, a visual shortcut with an unmatched capacity to touch the mind. They are easy to share – which also makes them a prime target. But images act as a revelator of something deeper. More often than not, the real target behind the cartoon is the media that published it. Are we going to put up warnings, the way we do on cigarette packs? "Satire can hurt your feelings!" Political cartoons and opinions are meant to provoke, yes, but above all they are meant to be thought-provoking. In this day and age, anything can make someone feel offended. And we tend to confuse feeling offended with being attacked. Humor is not about pushing others down, it's actually an incredible conflict-resolution tool. And freedom of expression is not incompatible with dialogue, and listening to each other. But it is incompatible with intolerance.

Do we want to wake up tomorrow in a sanitized world where satire becomes impossible? Because when political pressure meets political correctness, freedom of speech perishes.

"*The power of images has never been so big.*"

When I moved to New York in 1995 at twenty-something, I had a crazy dream: I would convince the (historically reluctant) *New York Times* to feature political cartoons. An art director told me: "We will never have those." But I was stubborn. For years, I did illustrations for them, then persuaded the Paris-based *International Herald Tribune* to hire an in-house political cartoonist. By 2013, when the *Times* had fully incorporated the *IHT*, there I was: featured on the *NYT* website and in its international print editions. We started translating cartoons in Spanish and Chinese. Only the U.S. print edition remained the last frontier. I had come back through the back door

and proven that art director wrong: *The New York Times* did have its own political cartoons. For a while in history, they dared.

Curiously, I remain positive. This is the era of images. In a world of short attention span, their power has never been so big. Out there is a whole world of possibilities, not only in editorial cartooning, still or animated, but also in new fields like on-stage illustrated presentations and long-form comics reportage – of which I have been a proponent for the last 25 years. The time has come for media outlets to renew themselves and reach out to new audiences. And stop being afraid of the angry mob.

We humans need humor as much as the air we breathe. Satire rides along with freedom. This is why extremists, strongmen and dictators, and the all ideologues of the world, can not stand humor. In the insane world we live in, critical thinking – with a smile – is more than ever necessary.

*The preceding text has been adapted
from an essay published in June 2019 on
chappatte.com, that received a global echo,
and from a TED talk posted in October
2019, "A free world needs satire."
(See ted.com)*

Cartoon published on the front page of *The New York Times* website on January 8, 2015, after the *Charlie Hebdo* attacks.

From the same author & publisher:
Another World, Oct. 2004 and March 2005
Globalized, February 2007
Partly Cloudy, November 2008
Signs Of Recovery, November 2010
Stress Test, November 2012
Slow Burn, November 2014
Democracy, November 2016 and February 2017

Chappatte's updated cartoons, comics journalism
and conferences : www.chappatte.com

Library of Congress Cataloging-in-Publication Data available : ISBN 978-1-62371-956-2

Publisher : Globe Cartoon, 1201 Geneva, Switzerland

Distribution : Interlink Publishing, 46 Crosby Street, Northampton, Massachusetts, 01060 USA

Order copies of the book from your local bookseller or by visiting : www.interlinkbooks.com

The cartoons in this collection were originally published on nytimes.com
and in *The New York Times International Edition*, except those
on pages 46, 55-56, 59, 76, 87, 92, 103-107, which appeared in either *Der Spiegel* (Germany),
Le Canard Enchaîné (France), *Le Temps* or *NZZ am Sonntag* (Switzerland).
Publication dates appear next to the images.

For permission to reprint a cartoon : e-mail cartoons@globecartoon.com

Layout : Sébastien De Haller, Atelier 109, CH-1205 Geneva
Printed and bound in Barcelona, Spain, by Beta